BROCK PURDY

The Journey Of a Little Star

From Small Town to Big Lights

(A Biography Book For Kids)

Deborah J. Stahl

THIS BOOK

BELONGS TO

Table of Content

INTRODUCTION

Brock Purdy wasn't always the starting quarterback for one of the best football teams in the world. In fact, for a long time, no one knew who he was. But, that all changed in a big way. It wasn't just his strong arm or his quick thinking that made Brock famous. It was his never-give-up attitude and his ability to stay calm, no matter how big the moment was.

You see, Brock Purdy didn't get the kind of attention that many other football players got when he was younger. People didn't expect him to be a superstar. He wasn't picked early in the draft like other big names in football. But Brock had something special—something that couldn't be measured by how fast he could run or how far he could throw a football. Brock had heart. He believed in himself, even when others didn't.

Let's step into Brock's world. Imagine being a kid who loves football. You play every day, throwing the ball around with your friends, dreaming about being on a big team. But, when it's time to go to college, you're not the first one picked for the team. You don't get the attention that some other players get. It would be easy to give up. But not Brock. He worked hard, learned as much as he could, and slowly started to make his mark. Little by little, he grew into a leader.

He played for Iowa State University, and it didn't take long before everyone started to notice him. With every game, Brock got better and better. He didn't just have a strong arm. He could make smart choices on the field. He could read the game, understand what was coming next, and help his team win. Brock's journey to success wasn't always easy. It was full of challenges. But through it all, he stayed determined. And that determination took him far. But being good in college doesn't always mean you get the chance to play in the NFL. It's a tough world, filled with players who are bigger, faster, and stronger. That's where Brock's story becomes really interesting. In 2022, the NFL draft came around. Many people didn't think Brock would be chosen. After all, many other quarterbacks were bigger names. But something amazing happened. The San Francisco 49ers picked Brock. He was the very last quarterback picked in the draft. Some people might have thought that wasn't such a big deal. But Brock saw it as an opportunity, a chance to prove that he was just as good as any other player.

He started his time with the 49ers as a backup quarterback. This meant he didn't get to play in the games at first. But that didn't stop him from practicing hard every day. Brock knew that one day if he was given the chance, he could show everyone what he was capable of. And guess what? That day came sooner than anyone expected.

In the middle of the season, the starting quarterback got hurt. The coaches called on Brock to step in. It was a huge moment. Imagine being asked to take control of a team with so many fans watching. A lot of people would be nervous. But not Brock. He stayed calm. He trusted his skills and his training. And when he stepped onto that field, he played like a true champion.

Brock led his team to victory. He didn't just win games; he made plays that everyone remembered. Fans started cheering for him, not just because he was winning, but because he was showing them what it meant to never give up. In a world where many people give up too easily, Brock became an example of what happens when you keep pushing forward. He showed that no matter how tough things get, you can always rise above it.

By the end of the season, Brock Purdy had become one of the biggest stories in football. He was no longer the backup quarterback. He was the hero of the team, and the fans loved him. But what made Brock even more special wasn't just his football skills. It was his attitude. He never bragged. He never thought he was better than anyone else. He just did his best, day after day, and let his actions speak for him.

Now, Brock is a star player for the 49ers. But he hasn't forgotten what it took to get here. He knows that there were tough days when he felt like giving up. He remembers how hard it was to be overlooked, to not be seen as the "big star."

But he also knows that by staying true to himself, by working hard, and by believing in his dreams, anything is possible.

Brock's story is one of determination, bravery, and hope. It's about doing your best, no matter how tough things get. It's about showing the world that being kind and humble is just as important as being strong and fast. So, if you ever feel like giving up on something, think about Brock Purdy. Think about how he stayed strong even when no one believed in him. And remember, if you keep going, you never know how far you can go.

Do you want to know more about him and how he became the hero of the 49ers? Well, don't stop here. Keep reading to discover all the amazing things he did along the way!

CHAPTER 1: EARLY LIFE AND FAMILY BACKGROUND

Brock Purdy was born on December 27, 1999, in the sunny state of Arizona. He was born in a small town called Queen Creek, and it didn't take long for his family to realize that he had a special talent. From the very beginning, Brock's parents noticed his energy and his love for sports. His dad, Shawn, was a former football player, and his mom, Carrie, was always encouraging him to follow his dreams. Brock had two brothers and a sister, and they were all close. Growing up, his family was everything to him. They would spend weekends together, often cheering on one another at different sports events, or just having fun outdoors.

Brock's family was a big influence on his life. They taught him the values of hard work, respect, and humility. His parents worked very hard to make sure that he and his siblings had everything they needed, but they also made sure to instill the importance of being kind and respectful to others. For Brock, these values were not just about being a good player on the field, but being a good person off it, too. Even as a young boy, Brock was known for being friendly and having a positive attitude. Whether he was playing sports or just hanging out with his friends, he always had a smile on his face.

When he was little, Brock loved to play all kinds of sports. Football, basketball, and even baseball were on his list of things he enjoyed. His parents never forced him into one sport, but they always made sure he had the chance to try new things. Brock had a lot of energy, and his parents encouraged him to find a sport that made him feel excited. Eventually, he found his true passion—football. He loved the feeling of throwing the ball, working with his teammates, and pushing himself to be the best. But, even though he loved football, he never forgot the lessons his family taught him about being a kind person and helping others.

Brock was only 7 years old when he started playing organized football. His dad, Shawn, was there to guide him through the early days. Shawn had been a football player, so he knew a lot about the game. He helped Brock understand the importance of practice, hard work, and focus. But Shawn also made sure that Brock was having fun. Football, after all, was supposed to be a game, and it should be something that made him happy. As Brock grew older, his skills improved. By the time he was in middle school, he was already one of the best players on his team.

At school, Brock was known not only for his skills in sports but also for his love of learning. He was a bright student, always paying attention in class and doing his best. His teachers noticed how hard he worked, whether it was on his homework or in group projects. Brock knew that being smart wasn't just about getting good grades—it was about learning as much as you could to become a better person. His family taught him that education was important and that if he worked hard at everything he did, success would follow.

As Brock got older, he started playing high school football at Perry High School in Gilbert, Arizona. This was a big step for him. High school football was a lot more competitive than the leagues he had played in before, and it was a chance for him to show what he was truly made of. At first, things were tough. Like many young athletes, Brock had to work hard to prove himself. But he never gave up. He kept practicing and practicing, and his dedication paid off. He worked so hard that, by his senior year, he became the starting quarterback for his team. He led his high school to many victories and helped his teammates grow stronger as well.

Brock wasn't just a good player—he was a great leader. He always made sure to help his teammates, whether it was on the field or off. He encouraged them to work hard, and he was always ready to pick them up if they were feeling down. His coaches saw something special in him, too. They saw a young man who wasn't just focused on being the best himself, but someone who truly cared about helping his team succeed. His teammates admired him for that. They looked up to him, not only for his skills as a quarterback but also for the way he treated others.

By the time Brock finished high school, he had built a reputation as a talented and hardworking football player. But even with all his success, he remained humble. He didn't boast about his achievements or think he was better than anyone else. Instead, he focused on getting better every single day. He worked with his coaches, spent extra hours on his passing skills, and studied the game to improve his understanding of how to lead his team. His work ethic was inspiring to everyone around him.

Despite his rising success in high school football, Brock knew that there was still a long way to go. He dreamed of playing football at the next level, in college, and maybe even professionally one day. But he didn't just want to play college football—he wanted to be a standout player who could make a real difference for his team. His parents supported his dreams, encouraging him to work hard and never stop believing in himself. They always reminded him that success didn't happen overnight. It took time, patience, and dedication. When it came time for college football, Brock was determined to go to the best school that would allow him to grow and improve. He chose Iowa State University. It was far from home, but Brock knew that if he wanted to reach his full potential, he needed to challenge himself. It wasn't easy. Moving so far away from home was tough. But Brock's family was there for him every step of the way. His parents made sure to visit him as often as they could, and they always cheered him on from the sidelines. His brothers and sister would call him to check in and tell him they were proud of him. These calls and visits reminded Brock that, no matter where he was, his family's love and support were always with him.

When Brock got to Iowa State, he quickly realized that college football was going to be a huge challenge. He was now competing against some of the best young athletes in the country. But instead of backing down, Brock worked even harder. He trained every day, watching films, practicing his throws, and learning from his coaches. Soon, he became known as one of the most dedicated and hardworking players on the team. It wasn't long before he earned the starting quarterback spot, and from there, his journey truly began.

His early life was shaped by the love and support of his family. They believed in him when he was young, and they never stopped believing in him, even when things got tough. It was their guidance and encouragement that helped him become the person he was—and the football player he would eventually become. Through every challenge and every victory, Brock always remembered the lessons his family taught him: to work hard, be kind to others, and never give up on his dreams.

As he looked back on his childhood, Brock knew that it was his family that had given him the foundation he needed to succeed. Without them, he might not have had the strength to overcome the tough moments or the courage to keep going. Brock's story wasn't just about his skills on the field—it was also about the love and support that helped him become the man he was. And that, he would always say, was the most important part of his journey.

CHAPTER 2: HIGH SCHOOL FOOTBALL JOURNEY

Brock Purdy's journey to becoming a famous quarterback in the NFL started when he was just a young boy. But it wasn't always easy for him, especially during his high school years. His story shows how hard work, dedication, and belief in yourself can help you overcome challenges.

Brock grew up in Arizona, and from a very young age, he loved sports. His parents encouraged him to try different things. He played basketball, baseball, and, of course, football. But football quickly became his favorite. He loved the excitement of the game, the teamwork, and the feeling of being in control of the ball.

When Brock was in high school, he went to Perry High School in Gilbert, Arizona. He didn't just start playing football right away. At first, he had to work hard to make the team. There were a lot of good players already on the team, and Brock had to prove that he deserved a spot. He worked harder than anyone else. He stayed after practice to work on his throwing. He spent extra hours learning about the game, studying other quarterbacks, and getting stronger. Slowly but surely, Brock made a name for himself.

He was a quarterback, but he wasn't always the tallest or the fastest player on the field. What he lacked in size, he made up for with heart. Brock was known for his determination. He never gave up, no matter how tough things got. If he made a mistake, he didn't dwell on it. Instead, he learned from it and tried to do better the next time. This made him a great leader on his team.

His teammates respected him because they knew he always gave 100 percent. He expected the same from them.

His high school coach, Mr. Sowers, saw something special in Brock. He recognized that Brock could lead a team, even when things weren't going well. Coach Sowers worked closely with him, teaching him not just about football but also about being a good teammate. "Football is about more than just being good at throwing the ball," Coach Sowers often told him. "It's about bringing your team together and making everyone around you better." Brock listened carefully to every piece of advice.

As a sophomore, Brock started to play on the varsity team. He didn't start as the star quarterback, but he quickly earned that spot. Every practice, he focused on improving his skills. He threw the ball, worked on his footwork, and learned how to read defenses. The more he practiced, the better he became.

By his junior year, Brock was already becoming a standout player. He led his team to the state playoffs, and his talent was impossible to ignore. He threw touchdown passes that left crowds cheering and defenders stunned. He had a natural ability to make big plays when the game was on the line. But it wasn't just his arm that made him great. It was his mindset. Brock was calm and collected, even when the game was at its most intense. He never let the pressure get to him.

The year was filled with unforgettable moments. One of the most memorable games happened during the state championship playoffs. Brock's team was facing a tough opponent, a team that everyone thought would win. But Brock wasn't intimidated. He threw a last-minute touchdown pass that helped his team win. The crowd went wild, and his teammates rushed to congratulate him. That game proved that Brock had the heart of a champion.

Brock's high school years were filled with ups and downs, but he never lost sight of his goal. He knew he wanted to play college football, but getting there wouldn't be easy. Many people doubted that a small-town quarterback like Brock could make it to the big leagues. But Brock was determined. He kept working hard, not just in football but in his studies too. He was determined to show that he was more than just a great athlete.

During his senior year, Brock's reputation as a quarterback grew. He was named the team's captain, and his leadership skills became even more evident. He worked closely with his teammates, helping them improve their skills.

He knew that a team wasn't just about one player; it was about everyone working together. His teammates trusted him, not just because he was a good player, but because he cared about them and wanted them to succeed too.

That year, Brock broke several school records for passing yards and touchdowns. His performance caught the attention of college scouts from across the country. But Brock never let the attention get to his head. He remained humble, always giving credit to his teammates and coaches. "Football is a team sport," he would say. "It's not about one person; it's about all of us working together."

By the time he graduated from Perry High School, Brock Purdy was one of the most sought-after quarterbacks in Arizona. His talent and leadership skills earned him a scholarship to play college football at Iowa State University. It was the beginning of a new chapter in his journey, one that would take him far beyond what he had ever imagined.

But even as he left high school, Brock never forgot where he came from. He stayed close to his family and friends, always remembering the lessons he had learned. He knew that his success wasn't just because of his hard work; it was because of the support of the people around him. And he was grateful for every step of the way.

Brock Purdy's high school journey wasn't just about football. It was about overcoming obstacles, proving people wrong, and always believing in himself. It was about showing the world that anything is possible when you have the right mindset and never give up. His story is one of hope and inspiration for kids everywhere, reminding them that no matter how big or small you are, with enough determination, you can achieve your dreams.

Now, Brock Purdy stands as an example of what hard work and perseverance can do. His journey from a high school quarterback in Arizona to an NFL star is proof that dreams can come true if you're willing to put in the effort. And it all started with a young boy who loved football and never stopped believing in himself, no matter what.

CHAPTER 3: COLLEGE FOOTBALL AT IOWA STATE

Brock Purdy's journey to becoming a star quarterback didn't start in the bright lights of the NFL. It started at Iowa State University, a school in a quiet town where he would grow into one of the most celebrated quarterbacks in college football history. The story of his time at Iowa State is full of hard work, determination, and the kind of leadership that would later take him to the NFL.

Brock's first year at Iowa State wasn't easy. He had been a star in high school, breaking records and leading his team to victories. But college football was different. The players were bigger, faster, and stronger. Brock wasn't sure if he could make the same impact at Iowa State. But he was determined to try.

When he first arrived at Iowa State, he wasn't the starting quarterback. He had to watch from the sidelines as the upperclassmen played. But Brock didn't let that stop him. Instead of being upset, he worked harder than ever. He practiced his throws. He studied the playbook every day. He watched the starting quarterback closely, learning everything he could. Brock knew that if he got the chance to play, he had to be ready.

That chance came sooner than anyone expected. During his freshman year, the starting quarterback got injured. Brock was called in to take over. It was a big moment, but Brock didn't feel nervous. He had worked for this moment for years. He stepped onto the field with confidence. He wasn't just playing for himself but for his team, his school, and everyone who believed in him. And right away, he showed just how talented he was.

In his very first game as the starting quarterback, Brock did something amazing. He led Iowa State to a victory over one of the best teams in the country. The fans were cheering, and his teammates were amazed at how well he played. It was as if all his hard work had paid off in that one game. But Brock knew it wasn't just luck. He had put in the effort, and now he was getting the chance to prove it.

As the season went on, Brock got better and better. He wasn't just learning how to throw the football. He was learning how to lead his team. Being a quarterback wasn't just about throwing passes; it was about inspiring everyone around you. Brock made sure his teammates knew they could count on him. He encouraged them when they made mistakes. He celebrated their victories. And when they lost, he helped them pick themselves up and try again.

His freshman year was just the beginning. By the time he was a sophomore, Brock had already become one of the best quarterbacks in the Big 12, the conference Iowa State played in. He was known for his strong arm, his quick decision-making, and his ability to stay calm under pressure. But what made Brock stand out the most was his leadership. He wasn't just the guy who threw the passes. He was the one who made sure his team believed in themselves, even when things were tough.

One of the most memorable moments of Brock's college career came in his sophomore year when Iowa State played against the University of Oklahoma, one of the top teams in the country. Iowa State had been the underdog in that game, but Brock had other plans. He played one of the best games of his life. He threw perfect passes, ran when he needed to, and led his team to a huge upset victory. That game became a highlight of his college career, and it showed everyone just how talented Brock was. He wasn't just a good quarterback; he was a great one.

But it wasn't always easy. Brock faced plenty of challenges during his time at Iowa State. He had games where nothing seemed to go right. He threw interceptions, missed passes, and sometimes felt frustrated. But no matter what happened, he always kept his head up. He always worked harder. He knew that football wasn't just about winning; it was about learning from your mistakes and getting better every day.

As his college career went on, Brock became the face of Iowa State football. Fans would show up to games wearing his jersey. They would cheer for him whether he won or lost. Brock felt the pressure. He knew that every game was important, not just for him, but for the people who supported him. But he never let that pressure get to him. He just kept doing what he loved: playing football, leading his team, and inspiring others.

His success wasn't just about his skills on the field; it was also about the way he handled himself off the field. He was known for being humble and respectful to everyone he met. Despite his success, he never let it go to his head. He took the time to talk to fans, sign autographs, and visit schools to talk to kids about the importance of hard work and perseverance. Brock knew that he had a responsibility to set a good example for the younger generation, and he took that responsibility seriously.

Throughout his time at Iowa State, Brock broke numerous records. He became the school's all-time leader in passing yards and touchdowns. He set a record for the most consecutive starts as quarterback. He was even named to the All-Big 12 team, a recognition given to the best players in the conference. But what Brock was most proud of wasn't the records. It was the way he helped his team. He helped Iowa State become a team that people respected, a team that could compete with the best in the country.

But as much as he loved playing football at Iowa State, Brock knew that his time there wouldn't last forever. He had dreams of playing in the NFL, and he knew that after college, he would have to move on. His time at Iowa State had been full of amazing moments, but he also knew it was just the beginning of something bigger.

When his final season at Iowa State came to an end, Brock looked back on everything he had achieved. He had grown from a young, nervous freshman into a confident leader. He had made a name for himself, not just as a great quarterback, but as a great person. He had shown everyone that anything was possible if you worked hard enough and never gave up. His time at Iowa State had shaped him into the player and person he is today.

And so, when the NFL draft came around, Brock was ready. He knew that no matter where he was picked, he had already accomplished so much. He had proven that with hard work, perseverance, and the right mindset, anything was possible. His college years at Iowa State had been the foundation of his journey, and they would always be a part of who he was.

In the end, Brock Purdy's time at Iowa State wasn't just about the wins and losses. It was about the lessons he learned along the way. It was about growing up, learning to lead, and finding his path. And as Brock moved on to the next chapter of his life, he never forgot the lessons he learned at Iowa State, or the fans who cheered him on every step of the way. His journey was just beginning, and Iowa State would always be a part of it.

CHAPTER 4: PATH TO THE NFL: THE 2022 DRAFT

Brock Purdy always dreamed of playing football in the NFL. But his path to the big leagues wasn't easy. When he was in high school, Brock was already a star quarterback. He worked hard, practiced every day, and led his team to many victories. His coaches and teammates saw his potential, and so did college scouts. He knew that if he wanted to reach the NFL, he had to do even more. He had to give everything he had, even when things got tough.

Brock decided to play for Iowa State University. It was a big decision. He wasn't the biggest quarterback. He wasn't the fastest. But he had something special. He had a strong arm, quick thinking, and, most importantly, he never gave up. When Brock stepped onto the field at Iowa State, he was ready to prove himself. His first year was full of challenges, but Brock faced them all. Every time he faced a new challenge, he worked harder. Every time he made a mistake, he learned from it. He knew that learning from mistakes was just as important as winning.

By the time Brock was a senior, he was one of the best quarterbacks in college football. He had broken many records at Iowa State. He threw more touchdowns than anyone before him. People began to talk about him. He was on the radar of NFL scouts. Brock was excited. He knew he had a real chance to make it to the NFL. But he also knew that getting there would be difficult. After all, so many great players were also fighting for a spot.

The NFL Draft is one of the most exciting and nervous times for a football player. It's when teams pick the players they want to join their team. The draft happens once a year, and only a limited number of players are chosen. Brock knew that only a few players would be picked in the first round. Players in the first round are often the ones who are expected to make an immediate impact on the team. The later you get picked, the harder it can be to make the team. But Brock didn't let that scare him. He knew he had the skills. He had worked hard for years to get to this point.

Still, the waiting was tough. The NFL Draft started, and the first few rounds went by. Every team was picking their players, one by one. Brock wasn't picked in the first round. Or the second. Or the third. He kept waiting. His heart raced as each round passed by. Would he get picked at all? As time went on, it started to feel like the dream was slipping away. But Brock never gave up. He kept believing in himself. He kept telling himself that his journey wasn't over yet.

Finally, it was the seventh round. This was the last chance for any team to pick a player. Brock's name had not been called yet. He was still waiting, but he was nervous. What would happen now? Would he be picked? Then, finally, the call came. The San Francisco 49ers had selected Brock Purdy. He couldn't believe it! He was going to the NFL! It was a dream come true. Even though Brock was picked last in the draft, he didn't let that stop him. He was excited. He was proud.

Getting picked in the seventh round didn't mean that Brock's journey was over. In some ways, it meant that his journey was just beginning. Being picked last in the draft is not easy. People often think that players picked later won't have as much chance to succeed. But Brock wasn't like the others. He didn't care when he was picked. What mattered to him was that he was given the chance to prove himself. And he was going to make the most of that chance.

When Brock arrived at the 49ers' training camp, he wasn't sure what to expect. He knew he was up against many talented players. Some of them were older and had more experience than him. But he didn't let that scare him. He was ready to show everyone what he could do. Every day, he worked hard. He studied the playbook. He practiced with his teammates. He asked questions. He listened carefully to his coaches. Even when things were difficult, Brock kept working. He stayed focused. He kept improving every day.

The 49ers started the season with a different starting quarterback. But Brock knew that if he kept working hard, he could get his chance. He didn't worry about what other people were saying. He focused on himself. And then, one day, the opportunity came. The starting quarterback got injured. It was Brock's time to step in. It was his time to shine. When he took the field for the first time, it was a big moment. He was nervous, but he was also excited. He knew that this was his chance to show everyone what he was made of.

Brock did more than just show up. He played amazingly. He didn't just play for himself. He played for his teammates. He played for the fans. And he played for everyone who had ever believed in him. Brock didn't just manage the game; he won games. He led the team to victory after victory. His teammates were impressed with how calm and confident he was, even under pressure. Brock quickly became a leader on the team, someone who could be trusted in the toughest situations.

The story of Brock Purdy's path to the NFL is one of hard work, determination, and never giving up. Even when things didn't go the way he planned, he kept pushing forward. He kept working toward his goal. He didn't care that he was picked last in the draft. What mattered was that he was given a chance. And he made the most of it. Brock Purdy's story is a reminder to all of us that dreams don't always come true the way we expect. But if we work hard, stay focused, and believe in ourselves, anything is possible.

So, Brock's journey from college football to the NFL wasn't a straight path. It was full of challenges and setbacks. But every time something went wrong, he found a way to keep going. He didn't let failure stop him. And that's why he is where he is today – playing in the NFL and proving that dreams do come true when you never give up.

CHAPTER 5: BECOMING THE 49ERS' STARTING QUARTERBACK

Becoming the Starting Quarterback for the San Francisco 49ers was not an easy road for Brock Purdy. It took hard work, determination, and a lot of belief in himself. His journey from a backup quarterback to leading one of the most famous football teams in the world is a story of never giving up, even when things looked tough. Brock was drafted into the NFL in 2022, but not in the way most people expected. Unlike the top players who were picked early in the draft, Brock was chosen last, in the seventh round. Being the last pick meant that many people didn't think he was good enough to be a star in the NFL. Most players chosen so late don't even make the team, but Brock wasn't like most people. He was used to proving people wrong. Even though he was the last pick, he had a fire inside him. He wanted to show everyone that he could play at the highest level and be great.

After joining the San Francisco 49ers, Brock began as the third-string quarterback. That meant he wasn't even the backup. He was behind two other quarterbacks, including the starter, Jimmy Garoppolo. But Brock never let that stop him. He kept working hard every day. He learned everything he could from his teammates, and coaches, and from watching the game carefully. He practiced every throw, every move, and every decision, getting better bit by bit. He knew that he might not get a chance to play right away, but he was ready for when that moment came.

Then, during a game against the Miami Dolphins, something unexpected happened.

Jimmy Garoppolo, the 49ers' starting quarterback, got hurt. This was a big deal for the team. They couldn't afford to lose their starter. But there was a problem. The backup quarterback, Trey Lance, had already been injured earlier in the season. So, that left Brock as the next option. He was called to come in and take over. This was the moment Brock had been waiting for, but it came in a way no one expected.

Brock stepped onto the field, knowing that this could be his only chance. He had never been in this situation before, and now all eyes were on him. He had to be brave. He had to trust himself. He had to remember all the hard work he had put in. The game was intense, with thousands of fans watching. But Brock stayed calm. He didn't let the pressure get to him. He just played football like he had always done. He was focused on his job: throwing the ball, making plays, and leading his team. The 49ers won that game. Brock had stepped up in a big way.

The next game came, and Brock was still the starting quarterback. This time, he was ready. He had already proven that he could handle the pressure. Now, he had to show everyone what he could do. The team was still recovering from injuries, but Brock kept playing with confidence. Each time he threw the ball, each time he made a smart play, he grew even more. He was no longer just the backup. He was the leader of the 49ers' offense.

As the weeks went by, Brock continued to impress his coaches and teammates. They began to see something special in him. He had an incredible ability to stay calm in tough situations. He never panicked. Even when the 49ers were behind in a game, he didn't give up.

He kept fighting, kept pushing, and kept leading his team forward. His calmness under pressure became one of his greatest strengths. Brock showed the world that he was more than just a last-round pick. He was a quarterback who could win games and lead a team.

In one of his first starts, Brock played against the Tampa Bay Buccaneers. The 49ers had a tough game ahead, but Brock was ready. He played with such skill and poise that it seemed like he had been the starting quarterback for years. He didn't just play well—he led his team to a dominant victory. The 49ers won 35-7, and Brock was named the game's MVP. It was a big moment in his young career. The media, his teammates, and fans were all buzzing about how he had stepped up in such a big way.

His performance didn't just stop there. Over the next few weeks, he continued to lead the 49ers through one victory after another. He was not only keeping the team in the game, but he was helping them win games they might have lost otherwise. His leadership and focus helped the 49ers finish strong in the regular season, earning a spot in the playoffs. This was a huge achievement for Brock, especially since he had just stepped into the starting role.

As the 49ers made their way into the playoffs, Brock Purdy had already become a household name. He had gone from being the last pick in the draft to leading one of the best teams in the NFL. Fans loved him for his story. They admired his grit, his calmness, and his ability to handle pressure. They also loved how humble he was. Even though he was playing at an incredibly high level, he never acted like he was better than anyone else. He kept his head down and continued working hard, just like he always had.

Despite being a rookie, Brock quickly became the heart of the 49ers' offense. His teammates trusted him. They believed in him. They knew that no matter what happened, Brock would give everything he had. And it wasn't just his skills that made him special. It was his attitude. He was always positive, always encouraging his teammates. He knew that football wasn't just about individual glory—it was about working together as a team. Brock Purdy wasn't just leading a football team. He was helping build something much bigger: a family of players who worked together for a common goal.

Through all the ups and downs, through every touchdown and every difficult moment, Brock Purdy kept proving that he belonged. He had faced so many challenges to get to this point, but he never gave up. From being the last pick in the draft to becoming the starting quarterback for the

49ers, Brock's journey showed the world that with hard work, determination, and a never-give-up attitude, anything is possible.

Brock's story is not just one of football. It's about believing in yourself even when others doubt you. It's about working hard and not letting any obstacle stop you from achieving your dreams. He showed everyone that it doesn't matter where you start—it only matters where you finish. And Brock Purdy was just getting started.

CHAPTER 6: AWARDS AND RECOGNITIONS

Brock Purdy's journey from a young boy with big dreams to a rising star in the NFL is filled with awards, recognitions, and moments that inspire everyone who hears his story. As a kid, Brock loved playing football and always dreamed of one day playing for a big team. He worked hard every day, always practicing, always getting better. As he grew, so did his skills, and soon enough, his name started to pop up in the news, first in high school, then in college, and finally in the NFL. Every time he earned an award or recognition, it wasn't just about winning something – it was about the dedication, heart, and passion he poured into everything he did.

Brock's very first taste of recognition came when he was in high school. As the starting quarterback for Perry High School, he led his team to victory after victory. He wasn't the biggest or the fastest player on the field, but what set him apart was his determination. He didn't back down from challenges and always stayed focused on the goal. That kind of attitude didn't go unnoticed. He became one of the top quarterbacks in his state, earning all-state honors in his senior year. These early awards showed that Brock was ready for bigger challenges. But he knew this was only the beginning.

After high school, Brock's path took him to Iowa State University, where he became the starting quarterback. Right from the start, he proved that he was more than ready for college football. In his very first season, Brock set records and led Iowa State to its first major bowl game appearance in years. He was not just a talented player; he was a leader who inspired his teammates. In 2019, he earned a spot on the All-Big 12 Conference Team. This was a huge achievement because it meant that Brock was one of the best quarterbacks in his entire conference, which included some of the top teams in college football. He didn't stop there. Over the next few years, he broke even more records, becoming the all-time leader in passing yards, completions, and touchdowns for Iowa State.

But perhaps the most important recognition Brock received in college wasn't about the numbers on a scoreboard. It was about his ability to lead his team, even in the hardest moments. The players and coaches saw him as someone who could be counted on when everything seemed impossible. Brock earned the prestigious title of team captain, which meant that his teammates believed in him more than anyone else. Being a captain wasn't just about playing well; it was about being a role model, showing the team how to stay positive even when things weren't going right. Brock showed up to every practice with the same energy, no matter how tired or frustrated he might have been. His leadership helped Iowa State reach new heights.

In 2022, after college, Brock entered the NFL Draft. He wasn't expected to go high in the draft, and many people overlooked him. But the San Francisco 49ers saw something special in him. They took him in the seventh round, which, at the time, didn't seem like a big deal. Brock knew he had to prove himself, and that's exactly what he did. His journey to the NFL was different from most players. While others around him might have had the fame and the spotlight,

Brock was determined to make his name known. He wasn't going to let anything hold him back.

Brork's big chance came in December 2022 when, due to injuries to the team's starting quarterbacks, he was called in as a backup. The 49ers needed someone to step in, and Brock did more than just step in – he took charge. In his very first game as a starter, Brock led the 49ers to a victory against the Miami Dolphins. He didn't just play well; he played with confidence and composure as if he had been doing this his whole life. The world started to notice.

By the time the 2022 season ended, Brock Purdy had already earned the nickname "Mr. Irrelevant" – a playful title given to the very last pick in the NFL Draft. But by then, he had proven that he was anything but irrelevant. He won five straight games as a starter, leading the 49ers to the NFC Championship game. That was an incredible achievement, and it earned him the respect of NFL fans and players alike. His ability to stay calm, lead his team, and perform under pressure made him an instant star. Brock became the first rookie quarterback in NFL history to win his first five starts, and he did so while leading his team to the NFC Championship.

In 2023, Brock's recognition grew even bigger. He was named the NFC Offensive Player of the Week after a spectacular performance against the Seattle Seahawks, where he threw for multiple touchdowns and led his team to a big win. His performances didn't just impress his teammates; they caught the eyes of coaches, players, and sports analysts all over the country. He was a leader not just by title, but by action. The 49ers went on a winning streak that made Brock one of the most talked-about quarterbacks in the NFL.

Brock's hard work and skill didn't go unnoticed by award-giving organizations, either. In 2023, he was named the NFC Championship Game MVP, recognizing his outstanding play in the game that helped push the 49ers closer to the Super Bowl. Although the 49ers didn't win the Super Bowl that year, Brock's performance in the playoffs made it clear that he was a player to watch for the future. Despite being a rookie, he had earned a reputation as a quarterback who could handle the pressure of the biggest moments.

Brock's recognition wasn't just about the games he played. His story was one of perseverance and never giving up, and that made him an inspiration to many. Young athletes looked up to him because he was a living example of how hard work pays off. It didn't matter that he was overlooked in the NFL Draft or that he wasn't considered the top pick. What mattered was that he kept believing in himself, even when no one else did. That message of resilience was just as important as any award he could ever win.

Outside of football, Brock's recognition also grew through his work in the community. He was involved in various charity events, helping young athletes who faced challenges similar to those he had faced. Brock understood how important it was to give back and inspire the next generation of kids who dreamed of playing football. His story became a lesson in how hard work, patience, and heart could take you far, no matter where you started.

In 2024, Brock Purdy continues to earn recognition and accolades for his performance both on and off the field. While his journey is still unfolding, it's clear that he has already achieved so much. He is a role model for young athletes everywhere, and his story will continue to inspire kids who dream of one day making it big. Awards and recognitions are just one part of his journey, but they serve as a reminder of the power of perseverance, leadership, and believing in yourself no matter what obstacles come your way.

Brock Purdy's name will continue to be remembered for the hard work and the passion he brings to the game. And though he's still just starting his career, his awards and recognitions already paint the picture of a young man who has made a lasting impact in the world of football. So, the next time you see him play, remember that every touchdown, every victory, every award, and every recognition he receives is the result of a journey filled with dedication, heart, and the unshakable belief that anything is possible if you never give up.

CHAPTER 7: PASSIONS BEYOND FOOTBALL

Brock Purdy is a football star, but there is so much more to him than just the game. Many people see him as the quarterback for the San Francisco 49ers, leading his team to victory. But if you look closely, you'll find that Brock is someone who cares deeply about things beyond football. He is a person who has passions that go beyond the field, and that makes him even more special.

One of Brock's biggest passions is his family. He talks about them all the time. His family has been with him through every step of his journey. They are his biggest fans, and he is theirs. When Brock was growing up, his parents, who both love sports, always encouraged him to do his best, no matter what. They made sure he stayed grounded and reminded him to keep working hard. It was his family who made sure he knew that winning on the field was great, but being a good person was even more important.

Brock loves spending time with his family. Even though his life is full of football practices, games, and travel, he makes sure to find time for them. He enjoys simple things, like going out to dinner with his parents or having movie nights with his brothers. They all laugh together, talk about life, and sometimes even play video games. Those moments away from football are some of his happiest times.

Besides his family, Brock has another passion—giving back to his community. He knows that not everyone has the same opportunities he had growing up. So, he uses his platform as a football player to help others. He often participates in charity events and has been involved in many fundraising efforts. One of the causes he cares most about is helping children who are facing tough challenges. Brock knows what it's like to work hard and fight for your dreams, and he wants to give those kids the chance to do the same.

Brock has visited children in hospitals, spending time with them and making them smile. He listens to their stories, encourages them, and tells them that they can overcome anything. To Brock, it's not just about football—it's about spreading hope and showing kindness. Sometimes, he even invites kids to football games, making them feel like part of his team. He loves to see the joy on their faces when they get to meet him and watch a game up close.

Football is a team sport, but Brock knows that teamwork isn't just about the people on the field.

It's also about the people around you—the coaches, the fans, and the people who support you behind the scenes. That's why he's always ready to give back to those who have helped him. He has done work with youth football camps, where he teaches kids how to play the game he loves. But more than that, he teaches them lessons about life. He tells them that being kind, honest, and hardworking is just as important as being a great player.

Another big part of Brock's life is his faith. He believes strongly in his values and lets his beliefs guide him in everything he does. Brock talks about his faith openly, saying that it helps him stay grounded and focused. It's part of the reason he's always so calm, even when things get tough. His faith gives him strength, and he is always looking for ways to grow as a person, not just as a football player.

Outside of football, Brock loves the outdoors. Growing up in Arizona, he spent a lot of time in nature. Whether it's going for hikes in the mountains or fishing by a quiet lake, Brock enjoys peaceful moments away from the noise of the world. He loves being surrounded by the beauty of nature, feeling the fresh air, and listening to the sounds of birds or rushing water. It's his way of relaxing and recharging, so he can be ready for the next big challenge.

He also loves animals, especially dogs. Brock has talked about how much joy his pets bring him. He loves playing with them and taking them on walks. Having a dog is one of the simple pleasures in his life. It reminds him of the importance of being gentle and caring. When you love animals, you learn how to be patient and kind. Brock carries these lessons with him in all areas of his life.

Another passion of Brock's is helping other athletes. He knows how much hard work it takes to make it to the top. That's why he spends time mentoring younger players, teaching them about football and how to stay focused on their goals. He wants them to know that success doesn't happen overnight. It takes effort, practice, and, most importantly, a positive attitude. Brock often shares his own story with them, telling them how he wasn't always the most popular or the most talented player. But he never gave up, and that's what got him to where he is today.

One of the coolest things about Brock is his love for learning. While many people know him as a football player, he is also a student of the game. He studies plays, watches films, and is always looking for ways to improve. He believes that learning is a lifelong journey and that you can always get better if you put in the effort. This love for learning extends beyond football. Brock is always curious about the world around him, always asking questions and seeking out new experiences. He knows that there's always something new to learn, whether it's about the game, the world, or himself.

Brock's love for the game of football is clear, but what makes him truly special is how he uses his platform for good. He doesn't just play for fame or fortune. He plays to inspire others. He wants kids, especially those who may not have it easy, to see him and know that anything is possible. He wants them to understand that it's not just about being the best player—it's about being the best person you can be.

In his free time, Brock enjoys reading books. He says that reading helps him stay calm and keeps his mind sharp. He likes to read about different cultures and the world around him, learning about people's lives and experiences. Brock believes that reading helps him connect with others and understand the world better. He is always looking to grow, and reading is one of the ways he does it.

Brock's journey has shown him the importance of being well-rounded. While football is a huge part of his life, he knows that life is about balance. He believes in working hard, but he also believes in taking time to enjoy the little things. Whether it's spending time with family, helping others, or just enjoying a quiet day outdoors, Brock knows that life is about more than just winning. It's about making a difference, being kind, and always striving to be a better version of yourself.

As Brock continues his career, he knows that football won't last forever. But the lessons he's learned and the relationships he's built will stay with him for a lifetime. Whether he's helping a child in need, spending time with his family, or enjoying the outdoors, Brock Purdy knows that passions beyond football make life full and meaningful. And that's what makes him a true role model for all of us.

QUIZ QUESTIONS

Early Life

1. When was Brock Purdy born?

A) December 15, 1999

B) December 27, 1999

C) January 5, 2000

D) November 10, 1999

2. Where was Brock Purdy born?

A) California

B) Arizona

C) Texas

D) Florida

3. What town was Brock Purdy born in?

A) Phoenix

B) Queen Creek

C) Mesa

D) Tucson

4. What sport did Brock Purdy first love to play?

A) Baseball

B) Basketball

C) Football

D) Soccer

5. Who was Brock's biggest influence in football?

A) His mom

B) His dad

C) His coach

D) His sister

6. How many siblings does Brock Purdy have?

A) Two brothers and one sister

B) One brother and two sisters

C) Two sisters

D) One brother

7. What did Brock's parents teach him about success?

A) To always play for fun

B) To work hard, respect others, and be kind

C) To win at any cost

D) To play alone and not trust teammates

8. How old was Brock when he started playing organized football?

A) 5 years old

B) 7 years old

C) 10 years old

D) 6 years old

9. What was Brock's first position in football?

A) Running back

B) Quarterback

C) Wide receiver

D) Linebacker

10. How did Brock's family support him in his sports journey?

A) They pushed him to be the best

B) They watched every game and cheered him on

C) They never attended his games

D) They only focused on his education

11. What did Brock's dad do before Brock started playing football?

A) He was a coach

B) He was a football player

C) He was a teacher

D) He was a doctor

12. What high school did Brock Purdy attend?

A) Gilbert High School

B) Perry High School

C) Mesa High School

D) Scottsdale High School

13. What position did Brock play in high school football?

A) Running back

B) Quarterback

C) Wide receiver

D) Kicker

14. What was one of Brock's key qualities as a high school player?

A) His speed

B) His teamwork and leadership

C) His height

D) His aggressiveness

15. When did Brock become the starting quarterback for Perry High School?

A) Freshman year

B) Sophomore year

C) Junior year

D) Senior year

16. Where did Brock choose to play college football?

A) University of Arizona

B) Iowa State University

C) University of Texas

D) University of California

17. What was Brock's major challenge when he first arrived at Iowa State University?

A) He was homesick

B) He wasn't allowed to play

C) The competition was tougher than high school

D) He couldn't get along with his teammates

18. What role did Brock play at Iowa State University?

A) Running back

B) Quarterback

C) Linebacker

D) Wide receiver

19. How did Brock's family support him while he was at college?

A) They never visited

B) They visited and cheered for him

C) They only called him once a year

D) They sent him to live with a different family

20. What is one lesson that Brock learned from his family?

A) Winning is the most important thing

B) It's important to work hard and be kind

C) Always play alone

D) Don't trust your teammates.

Awards And Recognitions

21. What high school did Brock Purdy attend?

A) Perry High School

B) Lakewood High School

C) Eastwood High School

D) North High School

22. What state is Perry High School located in?

A) California

B) Texas

C) Arizona

D) Florida

23. What position did Brock Purdy play in high school?

A) Wide Receiver

B) Quarterback

C) Running Back

D) Defensive Back

24. What recognition did Brock Purdy receive during his senior year of high school?

A) All-State honors

B) Best Player of the Year

C) Most Valuable Player of the Conference

D) Rookie of the Year

25. Which university did Brock Purdy attend to play college football?

A) University of Iowa

B) University of California

C) Iowa State University

D) University of Texas

26. What was Brock Purdy's role at Iowa State University?

A) Offensive Coordinator

B) Quarterback

C) Running Back

D) Linebacker

27. What major recognition did Brock Purdy earn in 2019?

A) All-Big 12 Conference Team

B) Player of the Year

C) Best Rookie of the Year

D) First Team All-American

28. In 2022, which NFL team drafted Brock Purdy?

A) New York Giants

B) San Francisco 49ers

C) Dallas Cowboys

D) Green Bay Packers

29. What round of the NFL Draft was Brock Purdy selected in?

A) First round

B) Second round

C) Seventh round

D) Fifth round

30. What nickname did Brock Purdy earn due to being the last pick in the 2022 NFL Draft?

A) Mr. Future

B) Mr. Irrelevant

C) Mr. Champion

D) Mr. Superstar

31. What was Brock Purdy's first game as a starting quarterback in the NFL?

A) Against the Seattle Seahawks

B) Against the Miami Dolphins

C) Against the Green Bay Packers

D) Against the Los Angeles Rams

32. How many games did Brock Purdy win in a row as a starting quarterback in 2022?

A) 3

B) 5

C) 7

D) 6

33. What record did Brock Purdy set in 2022?

A) Most passing touchdowns

B) Most games played as a rookie

C) First rookie quarterback to win his first five starts

D) Most yards thrown in a game

34. What award did Brock Purdy win in 2023 after his performance against the Seattle Seahawks?

A) NFC Offensive Player of the Week

B) Rookie of the Year

C) Super Bowl MVP

D) Player of the Year

35. What recognition did Brock Purdy receive for his performance in the NFC Championship Game?

A) NFC Championship Game MVP

B) Rookie of the Year

C) Super Bowl MVP

D) Best Leader of the Year

36. What team did Brock Purdy play for in the NFC Championship Game?

A) Dallas Cowboys

B) San Francisco 49ers

C) Green Bay Packers

D) Los Angeles Rams

37. What message does Brock Purdy's journey teach young athletes?

A) Winning is everything

B) Never give up, even when things are hard

C) Only the biggest players win

D) It's easy to make it to the NFL

38. Besides football, what does Brock Purdy enjoy doing?

A) Playing basketball

B) Community charity work

C) Painting

D) Writing books

39. What is one important quality that helped Brock Purdy succeed?
A) Speed
B) Leadership
C) Size
D) Strength

40. How did Brock Purdy earn the respect of his teammates?
A) By being the best at every game
B) By leading with confidence and showing up every day
C) By having the best statistics
D) By playing more games than others.

QUIZ ANSWERS

1. B) December 27, 1999

2. B) Arizona

3. B) Queen Creek

4. C) Football

5. B) His dad

6. A) Two brothers and one sister

7. B) To work hard, respect others, and be kind

8. B) 7 years old

9. B) Quarterback

10. B) They watched every game and cheered him on

11. B) He was a football player

12. B) Perry High School

13. B) Quarterback

14. B) His teamwork and leadership

15. D) Senior year

16. B) Iowa State University

17. C) The competition was tougher than high school

18. B) Quarterback

19. B) They visited and cheered for him

20. B) It's important to work hard and be kind.

21. A) Perry High School

22. C) Arizona

23. B) Quarterback

24. A) All-State honors

25. C) Iowa State University

26. B) Quarterback

27. A) All-Big 12 Conference Team

28. B) San Francisco 49ers

29. C) Seventh round

30. B) Mr. Irrelevant

31. B) Against the Miami Dolphins

32. B) 5

33. C) First rookie quarterback to win his first five starts

34. A) NFC Offensive Player of the Week

35. A) NFC Championship Game MVP

36. B) San Francisco 49ers

37. B) Never give up, even when things are hard

38. B) Community charity work

39. B) Leadership

40. B) By leading with confidence and showing up every day.

FUN FACTS

1. Brock Purdy was the last pick in the 2022 NFL Draft, often called "Mr. Irrelevant," but he quickly proved that being picked last doesn't mean you can't be a star.

2. Despite being a quarterback, Brock loves to play other sports, including basketball, where he is known for his quick feet and sharp shooting.

3. When he was younger, Brock always looked up to his older brother, Chubba, who inspired him to be competitive and never give up, especially when things got tough.

4. Brock once said that his favorite food is pizza, and he could probably eat it every day if he had the chance.

5. Before every game, Brock has a special routine where he listens to his favorite music, which helps him stay focused and pumped up for the match.

6. He's an animal lover and has a dog named Rocco, and they're often seen spending time together outside, enjoying the fresh air.

7. Brock is known for his love of adventure and often goes hiking in the mountains to enjoy the peace away from the busy football world.

8. One of his hidden talents is playing the piano, and while not many people know it, he can play several songs from memory.

9. Brock is very close to his family and often shares stories of how his parents and siblings are the ones who kept him grounded through his journey to the NFL.

10. Growing up, Brock had a dream of being a professional baseball player before deciding to focus on football, a decision that changed his life forever.

11. He's very humble about his success and always credits his teammates and coaches for any achievements, saying they are the real stars of the team.

12. Brock doesn't just focus on football during the offseason; he's a big fan of reading books, especially about leadership and personal development.

13. He's passionate about helping children who are going through tough times and often spends his free time visiting hospitals and youth centers to encourage them.

14. Brock's nickname, "The Purdy Boy," comes from his friends and teammates who say he plays the game with such style and finesse.

15. He loves the outdoors so much that whenever he gets a chance, he goes camping with friends, even if it's just for a weekend to relax and recharge.

16. Brock's favorite holiday is Christmas because he enjoys spending time with his family, exchanging gifts, and having big holiday meals together.

17. Despite his fame, Brock keeps his circle of friends small and prefers hanging out with people who've known him since before he became a star.

18. One of Brock's dreams is to someday become a coach or mentor, so he can pass on his knowledge and inspire future generations of athletes.

19. Brock once took part in a charity event where he helped build houses for families in need, showing that he's committed to giving back to his community.

20. He's a big fan of Marvel movies, and his favorite superhero is Spider-Man because he

loves how the character uses his powers to help others and do good.

Made in the USA
Las Vegas, NV
12 December 2024

13919522R00056